E♭ ALTO SAXOPHONE

CONCERT FAVORITES

Volume 1

Band Arrangements Correlated with
Essential Elements Band Method Book 1

ISBN 978-0-634-05205-7

HAL•LEONARD®
7777 W. BLUEMOUND RD. P.O. BOX 13819 MILWAUKEE, WI 53213

00860125

2

LET'S ROCK!

E♭ ALTO SAXOPHONE

MICHAEL SWEENEY (ASCAP)

MAJESTIC MARCH

E♭ ALTO SAXOPHONE

By PAUL LAVENDER

00860125

MICKEY MOUSE MARCH
(From Walt Disney's "THE MICKEY MOUSE CLUB")

Eb ALTO SAXOPHONE

Words and Music by JIMMIE DODD
Arranged by MICHAEL SWEENEY

March Tempo

00860125

POWER ROCK

(We Will Rock You • Another One Bites The Dust)

Eb ALTO SAXOPHONE

Arranged by MICHAEL SWEENEY

00860125

WHEN THE SAINTS GO MARCHING IN

Words by KATHERINE E. PURVIS
Music by JAMES M. BLACK
Arranged by JOHN HIGGINS

Eb ALTO SAXOPHONE

March Style

00860125

FARANDOLE
(From "L'Arlésienne")

Eb ALTO SAXOPHONE

GEORGES BIZET
Arranged by MICHAEL SWEENEY (ASCAP)

00860125

JUS' PLAIN BLUES

Eb ALTO SAXOPHONE

MICHAEL SWEENEY (ASCAP)

MY HEART WILL GO ON

(Love Theme From 'Titanic')

Music by JAMES HORNER
Lyric by WILL JENNINGS
Arranged by PAUL LAVENDER

E♭ ALTO SAXOPHONE

00860125

From THE MUPPET MOVIE

THE RAINBOW CONNECTION

Words and Music by PAUL WILLIAMS
and KENNITH L. ASCHER
Arranged by PAUL LAVENDER

E♭ ALTO SAXOPHONE

From Walt Disney's MARY POPPINS

SUPERCALIFRAGILISTICEXPIALIDOCIOUS

Words and Music by
RICHARD M. SHERMAN and ROBERT B. SHERMAN
Arranged by MICHAEL SWEENEY

E♭ Alto Saxophone

00860125

(From "THE SOUND OF MUSIC")
DO-RE-MI

Eb ALTO SAXOPHONE

Lyrics by OSCAR HAMMERSTEIN II
Music by RICHARD RODGERS
Arranged by PAUL LAVENDER

00860125

DRUMS OF CORONA

Eb ALTO SAXOPHONE

MICHAEL SWEENEY (ASCAP)

LAREDO
(Concert March)

Eb ALTO SAXOPHONE

JOHN HIGGINS

14

00860125

POMP AND CIRCUMSTANCE
March No. 1

Eb ALTO SAXOPHONE

By EDWARD ELGAR
Arranged by MICHAEL SWEENEY

00860125

STRATFORD MARCH

E♭ ALTO SAXOPHONE

JOHN HIGGINS (ASCAP)